SO-BFC-300

3 196 00208 5579

JAN 1 7 2013

STAGE SCHOOL

BROADWAY STAR

LISA REGAN

WINDMILL
BOOKS
New York

Published in 2013 by Windmill Books, An Imprint of Rosen Publishing
29 East 21st Street, New York, NY 10010

Copyright © 2013 by Windmill Books, An Imprint of Rosen Publishing

All rights reserved. No part of this book may be reproduced in any form
without permission in writing from the publisher, except by a reviewer.

Produced for Windmill by Calcium Creative Ltd
Editors for Calcium Creative Ltd: Sarah Eason and Vicky Egan
US Editor: Sara Antill
Designer: Nick Leggett

Cover: Shutterstock: Anton Gvozdikov bg, Liudmila P. Sundikova fg.
Inside: Dreamstime: Carlosphotos 12, Tom Dowd 27, Imagecollect 16;
Shutterstock: Margarita Borodina 20, Byphoto 7, Jaimie Duplass 3, 18, Helga
Esteb 6, Sonja Foos 5r, Gary718 14, Kojoku 22, Nodff 4–5, 9, 19, 28, Alexandre
Nunes 8, Paulaphoto 26, Perrush 23, Maureen Plainfield 15, Eduardo Rivero 21,
24, Joe Seer 17, Liudmila P. Sundikova 29, Lorraine Swanson 1, 11, Leah-Anne
Thompson 10, Vfoto 13.

J
792.028
REG

Library of Congress Cataloging-in-Publication Data

Regan, Lisa, 1971–
Broadway star / by Lisa Regan.
    p. cm. — (Stage school)
Includes index.
ISBN 978-1-4488-8092-8 (library binding) — ISBN 978-1-4488-8151-2 (pbk.)
— ISBN 978-1-4488-8157-4 (6-pack)
1. Acting—Vocational guidance—Juvenile literature. 2. Theater—New
York (State)—New York—Juvenile literature. 3. Musical theater—New York
(State)—New York—Juvenile literature. 4. Broadway (New York, N.Y.)—
Juvenile literature. I. Title.
PN2055.R44 2013
792.02'8—dc23

2012005287

Palos Heights Public Library
12501 S. 71st Avenue
Palos Heights, IL 60463

Manufactured in the United States of America

CPSIA Compliance Information: Batch #B3S12WM: For Further Information contact Windmill Books, New York, New York at 1-866-478-0556

CONTENTS

WELCOME TO THE SHOW!

Musicals are a magical world of dance, song, and show business. They combine acting, dancing, and colorful costumes with great songs and stories. The songs have wonderful tunes and clever lyrics (words), and the characters may make us laugh or cry.

On Broadway

Broadway is the word used to describe performances that take place in theaters along Broadway, a street that runs through the center of the theater district in New York City. The shows here are believed to be the best of all plays and musicals, which is why performers love to perform on Broadway.

➡ *Performers on Broadway put in long hours and a lot of effort.*

Fit and fabulous!

Broadway stars must be very fit to take part in a show. Shows often feature energetic dance and song routines, and stars may perform six nights a week for many months without a break.

➡️ *If you love singing, dancing, and being on stage, you could be a Broadway star!*

THREE SKILLS

Pop stars can sing, movie stars can act, and ballet dancers can dance. Musical stars have to be skilled at all three! Broadway stars are truly **multitalented** performers.

⇧ *The famous Hollywood actress Scarlett Johansson has appeared in a Broadway show.*

IN THE SPOTLIGHT

Scarlett Johannson
Famous as a movie star, Scarlett Johannson has also starred on Broadway in the play *A View From the Bridge*. A skilled singer as well as a great actress, in 2005 she also almost won the role as Maria in *The Sound of Music*.

Loud and clear

Starring in a musical is challenging. You will need to make sure that your singing is strong so that people can hear you clearly.

Hitting the mark

You must act the part, too, or the audience won't believe in your character. You'll also need to be a great dancer so that you measure up to the rest of the **cast**. Only the very best dancers and actors land the lead roles, so it is worth spending time working on these skills.

➡ *To make it on Broadway, you need to be trained as an actor, dancer, and singer.*

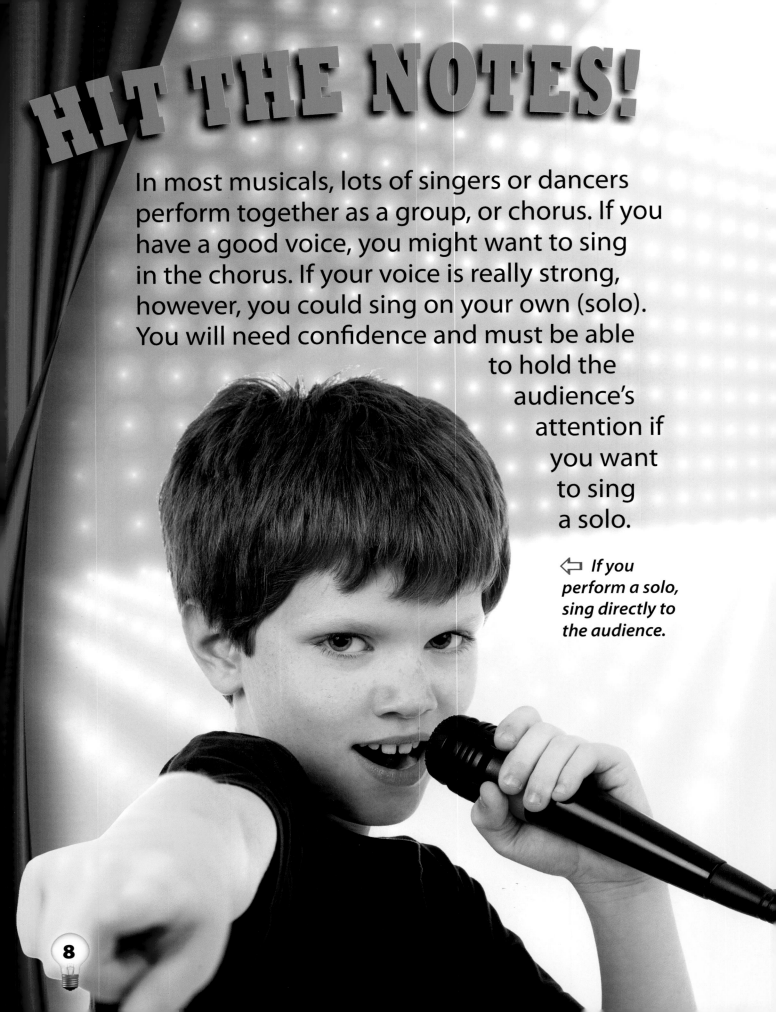

HIT THE NOTES!

In most musicals, lots of singers or dancers perform together as a group, or chorus. If you have a good voice, you might want to sing in the chorus. If your voice is really strong, however, you could sing on your own (solo). You will need confidence and must be able to hold the audience's attention if you want to sing a solo.

⇐ *If you perform a solo, sing directly to the audience.*

8

↓ *You may love being **center stage**, but being a good Broadway star means also knowing when to work as part of a team.*

BE A STAR

Listen up!

Listen to the director. He will tell you where to stand, when to speak your lines, sing, and start dance routines.

Stage picture

A good stage picture is when the audience has a clear view of everything they need to see. Upstaging is when someone stops you from being seen, or you stop someone else from being seen.

GET THE LOOK

A costume designer decides what everyone in the show is going to wear. He or she can be one of the most important people in a musical production. The costumes worn in a show help to create characters and tell the story.

Dressing up

Costumes can show whether the story is set in modern times or a long time ago, or if a character is rich or poor. Some shows, such as *Wicked*, have fairy-tale costumes. In *Spider-Man: Turn Off the Dark*, the stars wear modern clothes and also costumes based on the comic book's hero and villains.

⬇ *Musical costumes are designed so that performers can easily dance in them.*

Fancy costumes

Some musicals feature very fancy costumes. In *Beauty and the Beast* and *The Lion King*, some of the actors wear masks and outfits that make them look like animals.

⇧ *The costume designers for* Beauty and the Beast *won a Tony Award for Best Costume Design.*

IN THE SPOTLIGHT

Tim Rice
The words of the songs in *The Lion King* were written by Tim Rice. He is a very famous songwriter and has written the lyrics for 14 great shows.

FACE ON!

The first time you wear stage makeup, you might feel as if you have been painted! Stage makeup is much thicker than normal makeup so that the audience can see it, even from the back of the theater.

⇩ *It can take up to four hours to make up the actors in the musical* **Cats.**

Greasepaint

It gets hot on stage under the bright lights, so stage makeup has to be thick so it doesn't run. The base layer is almost as thick as lipstick and is called greasepaint.

Fantasy faces

Just like costumes, stage makeup is often bright and bold. In *Cats* and *The Lion King*, makeup was used to make the actors look like their animal characters. It took hours for the makeup artists to make up the actors' faces before each performance.

BE A STAR

Wipe it off!

Take care of your skin by removing all stage makeup after the show. Use baby wipes to remove the makeup, then repeat once more to make sure your face is thoroughly clean.

⇧ *Great stage makeup can transform the way that you look.*

ON STAGE

Being on stage is like being in a different world! A cloth, called a backdrop, hangs at the back of the stage and is often painted with a scene, such as a street, forest, or ship's deck. The backdrop for the show helps to convince the audience that the story is real.

⬇ *The backdrop can be painted to look as if some things are near and others farther away.*

Transformers

Some musicals use the small amount of space on stage in a big way. In *Wicked* and *The Phantom of the Opera,* pieces of the set are turned around or lifted up to make the whole stage look completely different very quickly. The stage designers and show director work together to make the best use of the space.

upstage left

upstage center

upstage right

center stage left

center stage

center stage right

downstage left

downstage center

downstage right

AUDIENCE

⬆ *The stage is divided into nine areas. This helps the actors know where to stand. It also helps the crew know where to place the props.*

Know your place

The director tells the actors where to move. It is really important that you know the stage directions, shown above, so you can quickly move to the correct place.

25

GET THE PART

If you want to be in a musical, you will have to **audition** for a part. The audition will test whether you are good enough. It is important to prepare for your audition so that you give it your very best shot.

Fitting the bill

The director will ask you to sing on stage so he or she can see if you have enough star quality to make an audience want to watch you. Even the best performers have to audition, sometimes more than once.

⬇ *Make sure you know your audition songs perfectly.*

⬆ *Choose a number from your favorite musical to sing at the audition.*

BE A STAR

To get ready:

- Learn at least one song that you love.
- Make sure the song suits your voice.

You could choose from these musicals:

- *High School Musical*
- *The Lion King*
- *Annie*
- *The Sound of Music*

THE BIG BREAK

Perform in as many shows as you can. Try to get parts in school musicals, drama group plays, or community theater shows. The more practice you get on stage, the more chance you'll have of making it into a Broadway show.

Making it big

If you're serious about being in a musical, you must aim high. Try to:

- Sign up for singing, dancing, and acting classes.

- Read websites about acting.

- Check local newspapers and the Internet for auditions.

⇩ *Many musicals have a large cast of children, so they are a good place to get stage experience.*

Play your part

Even if you don't make it into the cast of a musical, you could still play a part. There are many important jobs to do other than being on stage, such as creating the set backdrop or helping to make costumes.

▷ *Take as many roles as you can. Producers look for new talent in small shows, so if you are in the right place at the right time, you may get lucky.*

Child stars
More and more child actors are appearing in Broadway shows. The hit musical *Billy Elliot* had a total of 23 children in its cast!

GLOSSARY

audition (ah-DIH-shun)
To perform as a trial or test
to see if someone is right
for a particular part.

body language
(BAH-dee LANG-gwij)
Showing someone how you feel
just by the way you hold your body
or move your face.

Broadway (BRAWD-way)
The theater district in New York
City, famous for its bright lights.

cast (KAST)
All the actors in a production.

center stage (SEN-tur STAYJ)
The central area of the stage.

director (dih-REK-ter)
The person in charge of a play,
musical, or TV show.

modern dance (MO-dern DANS)
Dance movements that express
ideas and do not follow the same
strict rules as ballet.

multitalented (mul-tee-TA-len-ted)
Able to do many things well.

producers (pruh-DOO-serz)
The people who find the money
to make stage or TV shows.

project (pruh-JEKT)
To make sure your voice can
be heard from a distance.

props (PROPS)
In a play, musical, movie,
or TV show, objects that can
be moved by the actors.

street dance (STREET-dans)
Styles of dance often learned on the
street rather than in a dance studio.

upstage (UP-stayj)
The part of the stage that is
farthest from the audience.

upstaging (UP-stayj-ing)
Taking the attention away from the
lead actor or performer in a show.

voice coach (VOYS KOHCH)
A person who helps singers
and actors to train their voices.

FURTHER READING

Bedore, Bob. *101 Improv Games for Children and Adults*. Alameda, CA: Hunter House Publishers, 2004.

Levy, Gavin. *112 Acting Games: A Comprehensive Workbook of Theatre Games for Developing Acting Skills*. Colorado Springs, CO: Meriwether Publishing Ltd, 2005.

Nathan, Amy. *Meet the Dancers: From Ballet, Broadway, and Beyond*. New York: Henry Holt and Co., 2008.

Schwaeber, Barbie Heit, and George M. Cohen. *Give My Regards to Broadway*. American Favorites. Norwalk, CT: Soundprints, 2007.

WEBSITES

For web resources related to the subject of this book, go to: www.windmillbooks.com/weblinks and select this book's title.

INDEX